When You Were Young

A Memory Book for the Toddler Years

♥

Illustrated by Emily Boland

A Jane Lahr/Promised Land Production

Abbeville Press · New York

When You Were Young *was specially designed for you to record feelings,
thoughts, and important events during your child's third, fourth, and fifth years.
Throughout the book, passages intended for a specific parent are so marked,
inviting you both to participate in creating this original keepsake for your child.*

Editor: Amy Handy
Art director: Renée Khatami
Designer: Julie Rauer
Production manager: Dana Cole

First edition

*Copyright © 1991 Jane Lahr Enterprises and Promised Land Productions, Inc.
Illustrations copyright © 1991 Emily Boland. All rights reserved under
international copyright conventions. No part of this book may be reproduced or
utilized in any form or by any means, electronic or mechanical, including
photocopying, recording, or by any information storage and retrieval system,
without permission in writing from the Publisher. Inquiries should be addressed
to Abbeville Press, 488 Madison Avenue, New York, New York 10022. Printed
and bound in Hong Kong.*

Library of Congress Cataloging-in-Publication Data

*Boland, Emily.
When you were young: a memory book for
the toddler years/illustrated by Emily Boland.
p.   cm.
"A Jane Lahr/Promised Land Production."
ISBN 1-55859-164-8
1. Baby books.   1. Title.
HQ799.B65   1991*
649'.123—dc20   *90-43283*

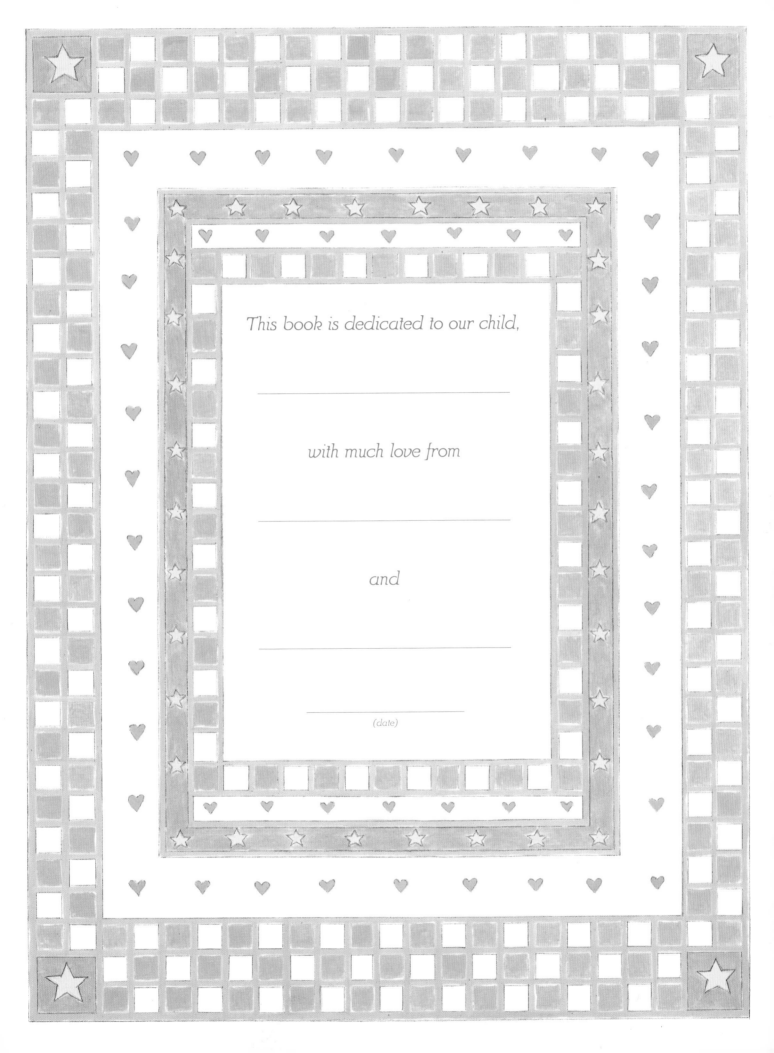

This book is dedicated to our child,

_____

with much love from

_____

and

_____

_____
(date)

CONTENTS

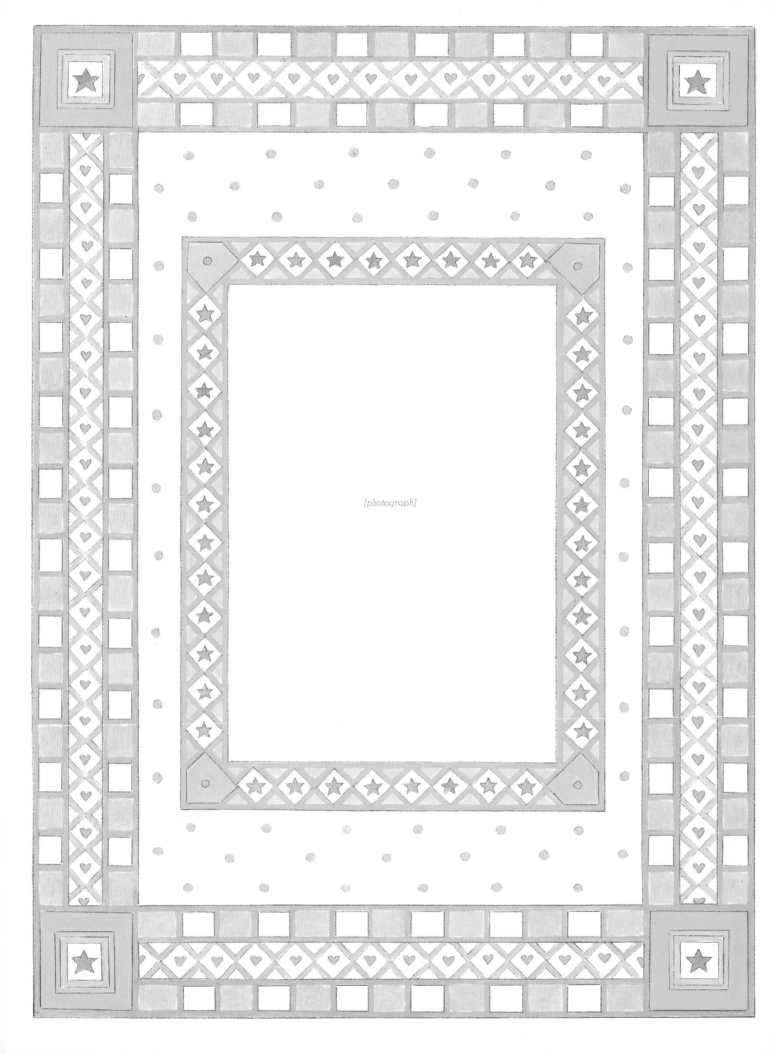

THE
THIRD YEAR

Height: _____

Weight: _____

YOUR FAVORITES

Your favorite foods were _____

_____, and

your favorite meal of the day was _____.

The games you never tired of playing were _____

_____.

Your favorite book was _____ by

_____. You liked it because _____

_____, and we read it to you _____ times a week.

Of all your toys, you liked _____

_____ the best. But when you wanted to snuggle, you

always reached for _____, your _____.

The first song you learned to sing was _____,

but your favorite music to listen to was _____.

10

Your favorite television show was _____,

because _____.

Your favorite video was _____.

At this age, what you liked doing best was _____

_____. On sunny

days, you liked _____; on rainy days, you

liked _____, and in the winter,

you loved _____.

Your favorite clothes were _____.

Your favorite pet was a _____ called _____, who

belonged to _____.

Your favorite playmate was _____,

who was _____ months old.

LANDMARKS

You began feeding yourself when you were _____ months old,

using a _____. Later on, you learned to use a

_____ as well.

You learned how to drink out of a cup when you were _____,

and you mastered a straw at _____. You gave up your bottle

when you were _____ months old.

You first began to undress yourself when you were _____.

The first things you learned to put on were your _____.

Then you learned how to _____.

You were _____ months old when you first put two words

together. And those words were "_____."

12

You started walking alone when you were _____ months old, but you first started to run when you were _____. You first learned to jump at _____ months, and to walk up stairs when you were _____.

You caught a ball when you were _____ months old, and you learned to throw it when you were _____.

Other things you learned to do this year were:

_____   _____
(Accomplishment)   (Date)

_____   _____
(Accomplishment)   (Date)

_____   _____
(Accomplishment)   (Date)

YOUR DAY

You got up at _____ in the morning, and the first thing you

did was _____. Your mood

was usually _____.

You would usually eat _____ for breakfast, and

_____ would sit with you while you ate.

You spent most of your day with _____.

During the morning, you would usually _____

_____

_____

_____

_____.

Your favorite lunch was _____, and

you would usually eat at _____ in the afternoon.

_____ would sit with you while you ate.

Right after lunch, you would usually _____

_____

_____

When the weather was nice, you would often _____

_____

_____

_____

_____ in the afternoon.

When you stayed inside, you would usually _____

_____

_____

Sometimes, for a treat, you would get to _____

_____

_____

15

Your favorite time of the day was _____

_____

_____ .

Dinnertime was at _____, and you often ate _____

with _____ or _____ with

_____ . While you ate _____

would usually sit with you.

After dinner, you liked _____

_____

_____

_____ .

Bath time was at _____, and what you liked most about

taking a bath was _____

_____.

You were ready for bed at _____ o'clock. Most evenings,

_____ would put you to bed by _____

_____

_____.

You liked going to sleep surrounded by your _____

_____

_____

_____.

MOM'S DAY

This is what I looked like this year; I was _____ years old.

[photograph]

I spent my day by _____.

Some of the things I enjoyed doing by myself this year were

_____.

My favorite movie was _____, my favorite

book _____, my favorite song _____.

The most important thing that happened to me this year was

_____.

DAD'S DAY

This is what I looked like this year; I was _____ years old.

[photograph]

I spent my day by _____.

Some of the things I enjoyed doing by myself this year were

_____.

My favorite movie was _____, my favorite

book _____, my favorite song _____.

The most important thing that happened to me this year was

_____.

SPECIAL OCCASIONS

HOLIDAYS

For _____, we gathered

at _____. The guests were

_____

_____.

You most enjoyed these moments of the day: _____

_____

_____.

On _____, we all got together at

_____. Staying for the festivities

were _____

_____.

The highlight of the day was _____.

We celebrated _____ by _____

_____.

We'll never forget the way you _____

_____.

Other occasions we'll always remember were _____

_____

_____.

Special parties this year were:

Date: _____ Place: _____

Highlights: _____

_____

Date: _____ Place: _____

Highlights: _____

_____

A PORTRAIT OF YOU

MOTHER

What I most enjoyed about being with you was _____

_____.

I'll never forget the day you said, " _____

_____." Or the day you did this: _____

_____.

I was proudest when you _____.

These were some things that made you laugh: _____

_____.

When you felt loving, you would _____

_____.

When you were frustrated, you would _____

_____.

You were funniest when you _____

_____.

22

A PORTRAIT OF YOU

FATHER

What I most enjoyed about being with you was _____

_____.

I'll never forget the day you said, " _____

_____." Or the day you did this: _____

_____.

I was proudest when you _____.

These were some things that made you laugh: _____

_____.

When you felt loving, you would _____

_____.

When you were frustrated, you would _____

_____.

You were funniest when you _____

_____.

Date:

Place:

Time:

YOUR
THIRD BIRTHDAY

We celebrated your third birthday by _____

_____

_____.

You wore _____,

and the cake was a _____.

The guests were _____

_____

_____

_____.

Special gifts you received were:

_____ from _____

_____ from _____

_____ from _____

_____ from _____

The best moment of the party was _____

_____.

What made the party special was _____

_____.

What you most enjoyed was _____

_____

_____

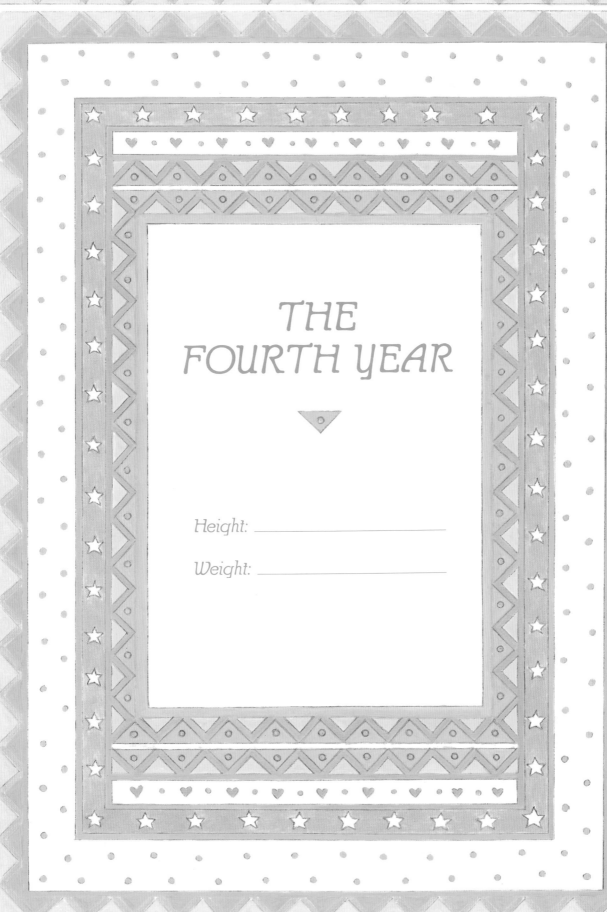

THE FOURTH YEAR

Height: _____

Weight: _____

YOUR FAVORITES

Your favorite foods this year were _____

_____, and you

liked this meal of the day best: _____.

Your favorite activity was _____.

Most of all, you liked to play with _____

_____. Your favorite books this year were

_____ by _____ and

_____ by _____.

You loved doing _____

by yourself. And what you liked doing best with us was _____

_____

_____

You liked listening to these songs best: _____

_____. And these were your favorite television shows

and videos: _____

_____.

At this age, what you liked to do on sunny days was _____

_____, but on rainy days you were happy to _____

_____.

Your favorite place to visit was _____,

and the people you liked visiting best were _____

_____ because _____

_____.

Your favorite pet was a _____ called _____.

YOUR DAY

You usually woke up at _____. The first thing you would

do was _____.

Then you would _____

_____.

You liked eating _____ for breakfast. Most

days, you would eat breakfast in the _____ with

_____. On the weekends, you would

_____.

You spent most of your day with _____.

This is how you spent your mornings: _____

_____

_____

_____.

You would eat lunch at about _____. Your favorite lunch

was _____, but you ate _____ with

pleasure as well. _____ would sit with you while you ate.

After lunch, you would _____

_____

_____.

When the weather was nice in the afternoon, you would usually

_____

_____

_____. When you stayed inside, this is how you would

spend the afternoon: _____

_____

_____.

On some days, you would have these special activities:

_____

_____.

Other activities that were important to you were _____

_____

_____.

You usually ate dinner at _____. You would generally eat

it with _____. You liked to eat _____

_____

In the early evening, you would spend your time this way:

_____

_____.

You still took a bath in the evening, but this year what you most

enjoyed was _____

_____.

Bedtime was at _____. _____ usually put you to

bed by _____

_____

_____.

You liked going to sleep surrounded by your _____

_____

_____

_____

_____.

MOM'S DAY

This is what I looked like this year; I was _____ years old.

[photograph]

I spent my day by _____.

Some of the things I enjoyed doing by myself this year were

_____.

My favorite movie was _____, my favorite

book _____, my favorite song _____.

The most important thing that happened to me this year was

_____.

DAD'S DAY

This is what I looked like this year; I was _____ years old.

[photograph]

I spent my day by _____.

Some of the things I enjoyed doing by myself this year were

_____.

My favorite movie was _____, my favorite

book _____, my favorite song _____.

The most important thing that happened to me this year was

_____.

PLAYMATES AND FRIENDS

Your best friend this year was _____, who

lived at _____ and was _____ years old.

You met when _____

_____.

What you most liked doing together was _____

_____.

Here's some mischief the two of you got into:

_____

_____.

Some of your other playmates during this year were _____

_____, who was _____ years old; _____,

who was _____ years old; _____, who was

_____ years old; and _____, who was _____.

These were some of the things you did with your friends:

_____

_____

_____

_____.

The time we'll never forget was when you and _____ did

this: _____

_____.

Some of your favorite adult friends this year were _____

_____

_____.

37

FAMILY TIME

Some of the things we enjoyed doing together this year were

_____

_____

_____ .

On the weekends, we often _____

_____

_____ .

In the winter, we would _____

_____ .

In the spring, we enjoyed _____

_____ .

In the summer, we would _____

_____.

In the autumn, we liked to _____

_____.

These were some of the best times we had together: _____

_____

_____

_____.

What made our time together special was _____

_____

_____.

SPECIAL OCCASIONS

HOLIDAYS

For _____, we gathered

at _____. The guests were

_____

_____.

You most enjoyed these moments of the day: _____

_____.

On _____, we all got together at

_____. Staying for the festivities

were _____

_____.

The highlight of your day was _____.

We celebrated _____ by _____

_____.

We'll never forget the way you _____

_____

_____ .

Other occasions we'll always remember were _____

_____

_____ .

Special parties this year were:

Date: _____ Place: _____

Highlights: _____

Date: _____ Place: _____

Highlights: _____

HOW YOU GREW

When you were _____ years and _____ months old, you were able to undress yourself completely.

You learned how to dress yourself when you were _____ years and _____ months old. First you learned to put on your _____, then your _____, and finally your _____.

You learned how to zip up and down when you were _____, how to button a button when you were _____, and how to tie your shoes when you were _____.

You started to choose what you wore each day when you were _____; your favorites were _____

_____

_____.

You were proudest of having learned to _____

_____.

42

Some of the things you liked doing by yourself at this age were

_____

_____

_____

_____

Things that you learned to do with others were _____

_____

_____

_____

Other accomplishments of the year were _____

_____

_____

_____

43

A PORTRAIT OF YOU

MOTHER

What I most enjoyed about being with you was _____

_____ .

I'll never forget the day you said, " _____

_____ ." Or the day you did this: _____

_____ .

I was proudest when you _____ .

These were some things that made you laugh: _____

_____ .

When you felt loving, you would _____

_____ .

When you were frustrated, you would _____

_____ .

You were funniest when you _____

_____ .

A PORTRAIT OF YOU

FATHER

What I most enjoyed about being with you was _____

_____.

I'll never forget the day you said, " _____

_____." Or the day you did this: _____

_____.

I was proudest when you _____.

These were some things that made you laugh: _____

_____.

When you felt loving, you would _____

_____.

When you were frustrated, you would _____

_____.

You were funniest when you _____

_____.

Date:

Place:

Time:

YOUR
FOURTH BIRTHDAY

We celebrated your fourth birthday by _____

_____

_____.

The theme of your party was _____

_____, and the decorations were _____

_____.

Everyone ate _____, and the cake was a _____.

You wore _____.

The guests were _____

_____

_____

_____.

Special gifts you received were:

_____ from _____

_____ from _____

_____ from _____

Games and activities at the party were _____

_____

_____.

The best moment came when _____

_____.

What made the day special was _____

_____.

Your favorite moment was _____

_____.

[photograph]

THE
FIFTH YEAR

♥

Height: _____

Weight: _____

YOUR FAVORITES

This year, your favorite foods were _____

_____,

and your favorite meal of the day was _____.

The things you liked doing best were _____

_____

_____.

Your favorite books this year were _____ by

_____, _____ by _____,

and _____ by _____.

When you were with other children, you loved to _____

_____

_____.

This is what you enjoyed doing by yourself: _____

_____.

And this is what you liked doing best with us: _____

_____.

Your favorite television shows were _____

_____.

Your favorite movies and videos were _____

_____.

You liked singing these songs: _____

_____. And

you enjoyed listening to _____

_____.

Your favorite place was _____.

The people you most liked to visit were _____

because _____

_____.

YOUR DAY

You usually woke up at _____. The first thing you would

do was _____.

Then you would _____

_____.

You liked eating _____ for breakfast. Most

days, you would eat breakfast in the _____ with

_____. On the weekends, you would

_____.

You spent most of your day with _____.

This is how you spent your mornings: _____

_____.

You would eat lunch at about _____. Your favorite lunch

was _____, but you ate _____ with

pleasure as well. _____ would sit with you while you ate.

After lunch, you would _____

_____.

When the weather was nice in the afternoon, you would usually

_____

_____.

When you stayed inside, this is how you would spend the

afternoon: _____

_____.

On some days, you would have these special activities:

_____

_____

_____

_____ .

Other activities that were important to you were _____

_____

_____ .

You usually ate dinner at _____ . You would generally eat it

with _____ . You liked to eat _____

_____ .

In the early evening, you would spend your time this way:

_____

_____.

You still took a bath in the evening, but this year what you most

enjoyed was _____

_____.

Bedtime was at _____. _____ usually put you to

bed by _____

_____.

You liked going to sleep surrounded by your _____

_____.

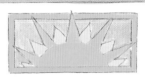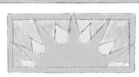

MOM'S DAY

This is what I looked like this year; I was _____ years old.

[photograph]

I spent my day by _____.

Some of the things I enjoyed doing by myself this year were

_____.

My favorite movie was _____, my favorite book

_____, my favorite song _____.

The most important thing that happened to me this year was

_____.

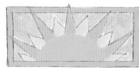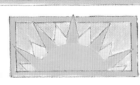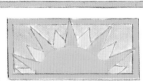

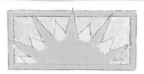

DAD'S DAY

This is what I looked like this year; I was _____ years old.

[photograph]

I spent my day by _____.

Some of the things I enjoyed doing by myself this year were

_____.

My favorite movie was _____, my favorite book

_____, my favorite song _____.

The most important thing that happened to me this year was

_____.

PLAYMATES AND FRIENDS

Your best friend this year was _____,

who lived at _____ and was _____ years

old. You met when _____.

You two could usually be found _____

_____.

Here's a story about the two of you: _____

_____

_____

_____.

Some of your other friends this year were _____,

_____, _____, _____

_____, _____, and _____.

The time we'll never forget was when you and _____

did this: _____

_____.

This year, what you most enjoyed doing with your friends in the
winter was _____

_____.

In the spring, you liked _____

_____.

In the summer, your favorite activity was _____

_____.

And in the autumn, you and your friends could be found

_____

_____.

Some of your favorite adult friends this year were _____

_____

_____

PRESCHOOL

This year, you went to preschool _____ times a week, from

_____ o'clock to _____ o'clock. The name of your school

was _____, and your first teacher was _____.

Some of your schoolmates were _____,

_____, _____,

_____, and _____.

This is what you did at preschool: _____

_____

_____

_____

What you liked best about school was _____

_____.

And here is a picture you drew this year:

FAMILY TIME

Some of the things we enjoyed doing together this year were

_____

_____

_____

On the weekends, we often _____

_____

_____

In the winter, we would _____

_____

In the spring, we enjoyed _____

_____

In the summer, we would _____

_____ .

In the autumn, we liked to _____

_____ .

These were some of the best times we had together: _____

_____

_____

_____ .

What made our time together special was _____

_____

_____

_____

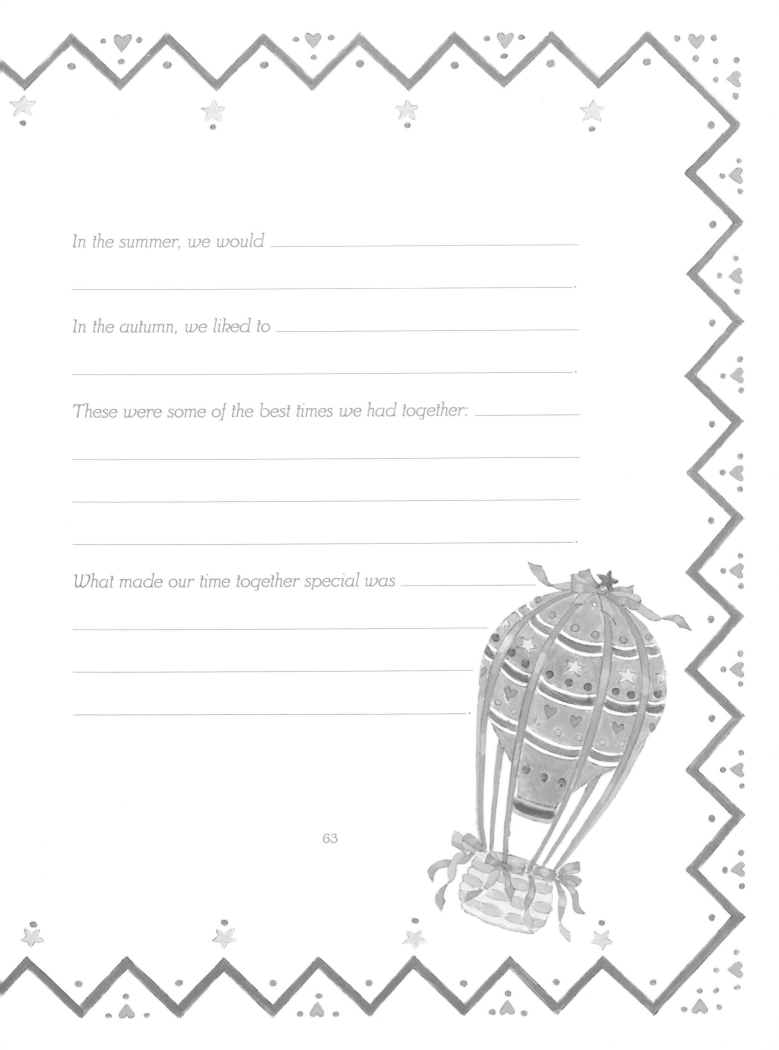

HOW YOU GREW

We were proud of you when you learned to _____

_____

_____.

You were proudest of having learned to _____

_____.

This year you started to help us by _____

_____

_____.

We knew how much you had grown when you _____

_____

1 2 3 4 5

6 7 8 9 10

You showed your independence by _____

_____

Among your accomplishments this year were _____

_____

_____

_____

67

A PORTRAIT OF YOU

MOTHER

What I most enjoyed about being with you was _____

_____ .

I'll never forget the day you said, " _____

_____ ." Or the day you did this: _____

_____ .

I was proudest when you _____ .

These were some things that made you laugh: _____

_____ .

When you felt loving, you would _____

_____ .

When you were frustrated, you would _____

_____ .

You were funniest when you _____

_____ .

A PORTRAIT OF YOU

FATHER

What I most enjoyed about being with you was _____

_____.

I'll never forget the day you said, " _____

_____." Or the day you did this: _____

_____.

I was proudest when you _____.

These were some things that made you laugh: _____

_____.

When you felt loving, you would _____

_____.

When you were frustrated, you would _____

_____.

You were funniest when you _____

_____.

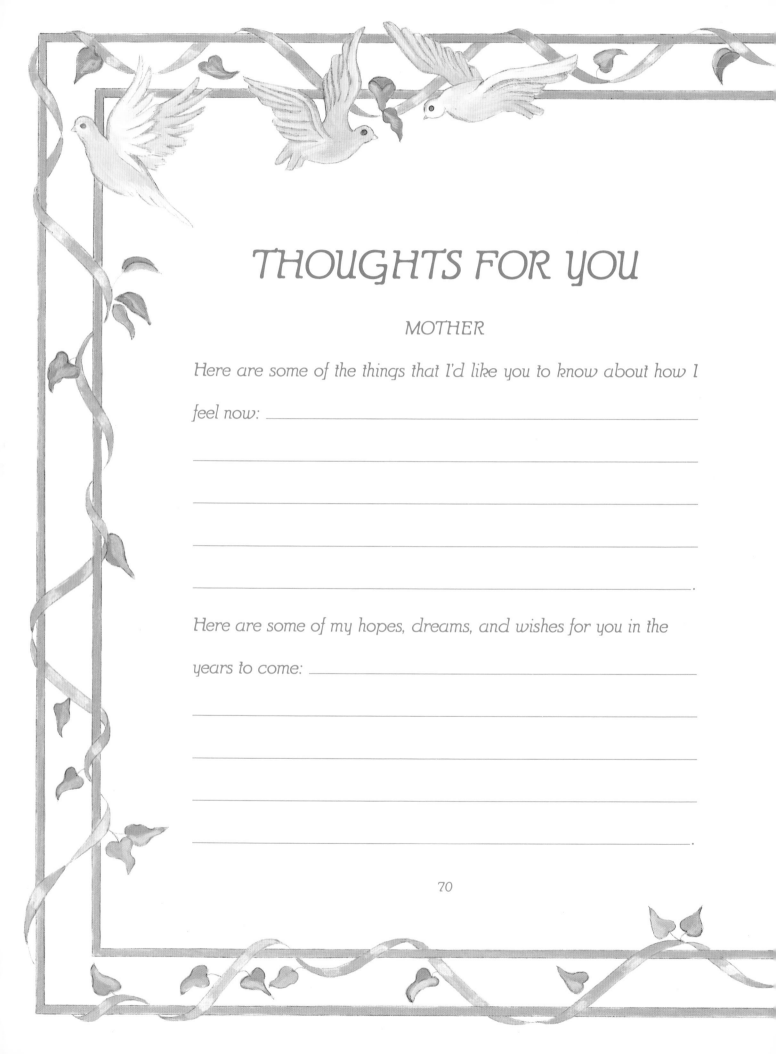

THOUGHTS FOR YOU

MOTHER

Here are some of the things that I'd like you to know about how I

feel now: _____

_____

_____

_____

_____

Here are some of my hopes, dreams, and wishes for you in the

years to come: _____

_____

_____

_____

_____

THOUGHTS FOR YOU

FATHER

Here are some of the things that I'd like you to know about how I

feel now: _____

_____

_____

_____

_____ .

Here are some of my hopes, dreams, and wishes for you in the

years to come: _____

_____

_____

_____ .